ROGER MCGOUGH ✪ BRIAN PATTEN

THE MONSTERS' GUIDE TO CHOOSING A PET

ILLUSTRATED BY GUY PARKER-REES

PUFFIN

PUFFIN BOOKS

Published by the Penguin Group
Penguin Books Ltd, 80 Strand, London WC2R 0RL, England
Penguin Group (USA), Inc., 375 Hudson Street, New York, New York 10014, USA
Penguin Group (Canada), 10 Alcorn Avenue, Toronto, Ontario, Canada M4V 3B2
(a division of Pearson Penguin Canada Inc.)
Penguin Ireland, 25 St Stephen's Green, Dublin 2, Ireland (a division of Penguin Books Ltd)
Penguin Group (Australia), 250 Camberwell Road, Camberwell, Victoria 3124, Australia
(a division of Pearson Australia Group Pty Ltd)
Penguin Books India Pvt Ltd, 11 Community Centre, Panchsheel Park, New Delhi – 110 017, India
Penguin Group (NZ), cnr Airborne and Rosedale Roads, Albany, Auckland 1310, New Zealand
(a division of Pearson New Zealand Ltd)
Penguin Books (South Africa) (Pty) Ltd, 24 Sturdee Avenue, Rosebank, Johannesburg 2196, South Africa

Penguin Books Ltd, Registered Offices: 80 Strand, London WC2R 0RL, England

www.penguin.com

First published in hardback in Puffin Books 2004
Published in paperback 2005
I

This selection text copyright © Roger McGough, Brian Patten, 2004
Illustrations copyright © Guy Parker-Rees, 2004
All rights reserved

The moral right of the authors and illustrator has been asserted

Set in Centaur 15pt
Made and printed in China by Midas

British Library Cataloguing in Publication Data
A CIP catalogue record for this book is available from the British Library

ISBN 0–141–31766–3

CONTENTS

THE ANIMALS ON MERCURY ARE SCARY

The animals on Mars smell like cheese
The animals on Saturn are hairy
On Venus they just sniffle and sneeze.

The animals on Neptune are fishy
The animals on Jupiter are cold
On Uranus they sting when you touch them
On Pluto they're too fierce to hold.

From Allura as far as Zozanza
We think it's a terrible shame
That none of the animals are cuddly
And certainly not house-trained or tame.

So we're leaving by spaceship tomorrow
And for planet Earth we are bound
For they say that's where the finest pets
In the universe can be found.

We've landed on Earth but we don't know yet
What kind of pet we should get.

Should it be a dog, or a snake beneath a log?
What kind of pet should we get?

A duck or a dingo? A lion or flamingo?
What kind of pet should we get?

2

Feathered or furry? Perhaps with scales?
Will it have horns or tusks or tails?

Where shall we look first? We'll give you a clue:
The animals cluck, quack, baa and mew.

3

THE PECKING ORDER

Charlie Chicken knew the pecking order,
He was as good as a good egg could be.
His father was tough and ruled the roost,
And it was plain for us all to see
Though they would never turn into swans
You couldn't fault them as poultry.

WHY DO SHEEP?

Why do sheep
have curly coats?

To keep the wind
out of their froats.

THE MOUSE'S INVITATION CARDS

'Come at seven,' 'Come at nine,'
'Come whenever you want.'
On the shelf the printed cards
Seem kind in their intent.

But the mouse will always stay at home,
He will never venture out,
No matter how the cards insist
Friends are all about.

One's from a cat, one's from an owl,
And both are intent
To draw him from his nest and then
Have him where they want.

THREE YOUNG RATS

Three young rats in satin suits
Three young cats in leather boots
Three young ducks in gaberdines
Three young dogs in denim jeans
Went out to walk with two young pigs
In miniskirts and orange wigs
But suddenly it chanced to rain
And so they all went home again.

CROCODILE FARM

Come with me
Down to Crocodile Farm
If you keep your eyes open
You'll come to no harm

There's the old milking shed
Where it's all done by hand
Though we've lost quite a few
As you'll well understand

We make crocodile butter
Yoghurt and cream
Though nobody buys it
It's all lumpy and green

High up on the pastures
They're put out to graze
Where they round up the shepherds
And worry them for days

Then we fatten them up
And kill them humanely
The ones we can catch –
They kill us, mainly

But crocodile meat
Is an acquired taste
A cross between sewage
And stale salmon paste

So I'm giving up crocodiles
Cos my account's in the red
And starting a farm
For alligators instead.

THERE WAS ONCE A WHOLE WORLD IN THE SCARECROW

The farmer has dismantled the old scarecrow.
He has pulled out the straw and scattered it.
The wind has blown it away.
(A mouse once lived in its straw heart.)
He has taken off the old coat.
(In the torn pocket a grasshopper lived.)
He has thrown away the old shoes.
(In the left shoe a spider sheltered.)
He has taken away the hat.
(A little sparrow once nested there.)
And now the field is empty.
The little mouse has gone.
The grasshopper has gone.
The spider has gone.
The bird has gone.
The scarecrow,
Their world,
Has gone.
It has
all
g
o
n
e

I ASKED A SCARECROW IN OUT OF THE SNOW

I asked a scarecrow in out of the snow.
'Please be a guest in my house.'

The scarecrow said, 'Can I bring a friend?
For in my sleeve lives a mouse.'

Into the house and out of the snow
Came a small mouse and an old scarecrow.

From another sleeve out popped a shrew.
'Excuse me,' it said, 'but can I come too?'

Into the house and out of the snow
Came a shrew, a mouse and an old scarecrow.

Then a tiny voice called from the straw,
'Is there room in your house for just one more?'

Into the house and out of the snow
Came a vole, a shrew, a mouse and scarecrow.

PET SCARECROW

A scarecrow's not the kind of pet
That anyone would want to get.
It couldn't jump or catch a ball,
Lick your face
Or come when you call.

Waiting for a hug
With arms out wide,
The scarecrow
Stands alone outside.

LOVE A DUCK

I love a duck called Jack
He's my very favourite pet
But last week he took poorly
So I took him to the vet.

The vet said: 'Lad, the news is bad,
Your duck has lost its quack
And there's nowt veterinary science
Can do to bring it back.'

A quackless duck? What thankless luck!
Struck dumb without a word
Rendered mute like a bunged-up flute
My splendid, tongue-tied bird.

All day now on the duvet
He sits and occasionally sighs
Dreaming up a miracle
A faraway look in his eyes.

Like an orphan for his mother
Like maiden for her lover
Waiting silently is Jack
For the gab to come back

For the gift of tongues that goes . . .

ODD DUCK OUT

It was really quite unnatural,
But a marvellous bit of luck
When on the banks of the River Thames
I saw a talking duck.

It stopped and said, 'Good morning,'
And asked me if I knew
Where it could find some chickens
To make some chicken stew.

'I thought you liked things cold,' I said,
'I thought you liked them raw.'
'I do, I do, I do,' it said,
And offered me its paw.

'I thought you had webbed feet,' I said,
'And hated chicken stew.'
'I do, I do, I do,' it said,
And then away it flew.

BAD MANNERS

It's extraordinary bad manners
And hard to justify
Picnicking near a pigpen
On spare ribs or pork pie.
You might be eating someone's granny,
Their father or their mum,
Those pork pies you're guzzling
Might be someone's chum.

WINIFRED WEASEL

Miss Winifred Weasel long and thin
All night sneaked around the farm,
Until she came to a narrow gap
Newly opened in the barn.

Winifred Weasel long and thin
Squeezed her frame neatly in!

Miss Winifred Weasel felt at ease.
She was quite amazed at all she saw:
She attacked the carrots and the cheese,
And kept one eye upon the door.

Winifred Weasel long and thin
Squeezed her frame neatly in!

Miss Winifred Weasel nibbled and gnawed.
Rotund, then fat soon she grew,
And when the mouse came it deplored
How she had eaten enough for two.

Miss Winifred Weasel long and thing
Squeezed her frame neatly in!

17

Suddenly outside the barn
She heard the noise of human feet.
She danced about in great alarm
But could find no way to retreat.

Winifred Weasel long and thin
Squeezed her frame neatly in!

She found the place where she got in,
But now the barn had become a trap.
She wished on her life she was still thin
And could squeeze out through that narrow gap.

Winifred Weasel once long and thin
Doomed by greed to be caged in!

THE LOVE-DOOMED RAT

O poor rat. Poor rat!
It's fallen in love with a cat! A cat!

O what will become of it?
It's hated enough for spreading plague and stuff,
It's hated enough!

It lives underground without the sun.
In its drab dark world it has no fun.

Poor rat!
The trouble it's taking to make itself clean!
It's so love-starved and lean!

I hear it say: 'My eyes are tiny
And hers are like the moon,
And soon, O soon I must risk it –
I must visit that cat's basket!'

What will become of it,
Struck by love to such a strange degree,
As lovesick as you or I could be?

WE'RE AFTER A PET BUT WE DON'T KNOW YET
What kind of pet we should get.

How about a bird?

We decided a dodo
Would be a real no-no
And a vulture wasn't on at any price.

And we knew that however regal
An eagle isn't legal
And an albatross would sink us in a trice.

Perhaps a parrot that could talk
So when you took him for a walk
Down the street to meet the folks
He could tell you lots of jokes.

We wondered if at a pinch
We should keep a goldfinch
A hummingbird a-humming would be nice.

So we went to have a peep
At all things that squawk and cheep
And live on seeds and juicy worms and mice.

21

BIRDS

You might know about the yaffle,
The culver and the widgeon –
All a bit more exciting than
That boring bird, the pigeon.

How about the cassowary?
The apteryx? The moa?
Those flightless birds next to whom
Most others run much slower.

There is nothing beats the eagle
Or the falcon or the kite,
When it comes to acrobatics
They excel themselves in flight.

Some other birds mistrust the sky
And think that water's grander.
I am thinking now of the swan,
The ouzel and goosander.

It is true the parrot's boastful
And speaks a lot of rot
And insists on being filthy
When his owners wish he'd not.

He's really not my favourite bird.
I suppose that at a push
My favourite bird would be the wren
If it sang more like the thrush.

Let's not say much about the dodo,
The poor thing is obsolete.
One reason is because it was
Baked by pirates as a treat.

Today the saddest birds of all
Must be the hen and the turkey.
Their dull lives are brief, their futures
Can look extremely murky.

In recent times the safest bird
Has become the cooing dove,
For who on this Earth will admit
To a taste for killing Love?

OSTRICH

One morning
an ostrich
buried his head
in the sand
and fell asleep.

On waking
he couldn't remember
where he'd buried it.

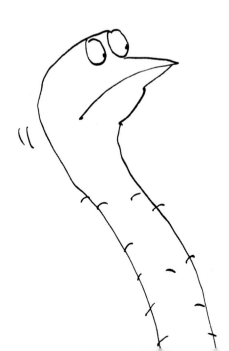

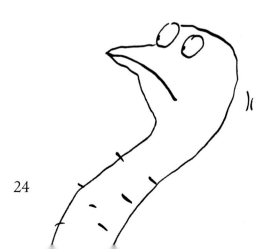

THE OWL'S TRICK

From its hollow and ancient tree
An owl looked down and said to me:

'About my feet are swarms of mice –
I can easily leave them there,
For from their feet I've ripped their toes
And now they'll not go anywhere.

'I eat them slowly at my ease,
I pick and choose them as I please.
The fattest one I let digest
Before indulging in the rest.

'I bring them corn into my croft,
It keeps them both alive and soft.
Before this trick occurred to me
They were nimble and scurried free.

'I've neatly torn the paws from each
Panicking creature in my reach;
No doubt you think I'm cruel, but then
Who invented the battery hen?'

SEAGULLS

Seagulls are eagles
with no head for heights

For soggy old crusts
they get into fights

Out-of-tune buskers
beggars and screechers

Seagulls are not
my favourite creatures.

BLUE MACAW

I used to keep
a blue macaw
in my bedside
bottom drawer

But he was never
happy there
among the socks
and underwear

He pined for sunshine
trees galore
as in Brazil
and Ecuador

Knowing then
what I must do
I journeyed south
as far as Kew

In the Gardens
set him free
(wasn't that
macawful of me?)

CROW

A crow is a crow is a crow
In the bird popularity poll
We are the lowest of the low
But do we care? No.

While others twitter on and on, or worse
Bang out the same three notes
Of musical Morse, we refrain.
If there's 'owt to caw, we caw.

Long since banned from the dawn chorus
We lie in bed until lunchtime
Then leisurely flap down
And bag a few smug worms.

Potter about in the afternoon
Call on friends, or simply bide.
For the night that others hide from
Is the time that we like best.

Nestled in treetops gently swaying
We stretch out to the sky
And hold court with the moon.
Stargazers we. The thinkers.

Looking deep into the heavens
We drift and drift and drift
Up and up into the blueblack
Into the very crowness of the universe.

A crow is a crow is a crow
In the bird popularity poll
We are the lowest of the low
But do we care? No.

THE DAFT OWL

Not all owls go
'Tu-whit, tu-whoo'

(It is not something
All owls do).

I knew one whoo
Was tu-whit

less

    tu-

       whoo.

THE MUSCOVY DUCK

Early spring, and out on the misty river
The poor old Muscovite is lonely as ever.
Winter's buried its companion.
It swims behind the mallards
Or sits near them on the shore,
An old uncle with nowhere to go.

STRANGEWAYS

Granny's canary
Escaped from its cage
It's up on the roof
In a terrible rage

Hurling abuse
And making demands
That Granny fails
To understand

'Lack of privacy'
'Boring old food'
It holds up placards
Painted and rude

It's not coming down
The canary warns
Till Gran carries out
Major reforms

The message has spread
And now for days
Cage-birds have been acting
In very strange ways.

CAGES ARE CRUEL AND BIRDS NEED TO FLY
So somewhere else we'll have to try
To find a different kind of pet.
Has anyone tried an insect yet?

Things that wriggle, crawl and creep
Are cheap to feed and easy to keep
As long as you don't let one wriggle
Inside your vest to tiggle your miggle.

32

Or, even worse, find a mini-beast
Who regards you as a mini-feast
Meals-on-legs three times a day
Until you're eaten all away.

But we'll find a pet that's right, I'm sure
Behind the creepy-crawly door.

33

A MOTH IN NOVEMBER

Poor old moth,
we mistook you
for a flake of ash,
a solitary scrap
blown about
by the wind.
Today's
a dark
cold day
in November,
but what use to you
the heat of the bonfire?

THE FRIENDLESS MOTH

A moth with a long and Latin name
One day flew into a flame,
But because its problems were not shared
No one minded much or cared.
There was no one on whom it could depend,
It had no family or best friend.
I buried it one autumn dawn
Beneath a leaf out on the lawn.
I hope to Heaven it will ascend
And up there find a decent friend.

THE APPLE-FLAVOURED WORM

When the rivers were pregnant with fishes
And the trees were pregnant with buds,
When the Earth was fat with seeds
And a million other goods,
Taking a snooze in an apple
Was an apple-flavoured worm.
It heard God's voice say, 'Bite.
Eve, it is your turn.'

When the sky was bluer than blue
And the Earth shone bright as a pin,
Before Paradise had been abandoned
Or a tongue had invented a sin,
Taking a snooze in an apple
Was the apple-flavoured worm.
It heard God's voice say, 'Bite.
Adam, it's now your turn.'

Then the bloom was gone from the garden,
The first petal had dropped from a flower,
The wound in the rib's cage was healed
And Satan had lived for an hour.

And wide awake in the apple
The apple-flavoured worm
Heard the Gates of Heaven closing
And a key of iron turn.

EARWIGS

Earwigs wear earrings
When going to the ball

Roaches wear broaches
Or nothing at all.

EAR WIGS

Fancy having wigs for ears
That's the craziest invention for years!

What next? A hairpiece for a nose?
Or toupees for toes, I suppose?

THE DELIGHTED FLY

A fly landing on a statue's nose
Said, 'This human in repose
Is cold and still. It's quite a thrill
To walk on breathless lips
And unblinking eyes,
To cross fingers that do not itch
Or wish to crush;
To rest on an adam's apple or
Circumnavigate without fear
The cool rim of an ear.
If all humans were like this I
Would be a happier fly.'

US FLIES IN HAMBURGERS*

If you go down the High Street today
You'll be sure of a big surprise
When you order your favourite burger
With a milkshake and regular fries.

For the secret is out
I tell you no lies
They've stopped using beef
In favour of FLIES.

FLIES, FLIES, big juicy FLIES,
FLIES as American as apple pies.

Horseflies, from Texas, as big as your thumb
Are sautéed with onions and served in a bun.

Free-range bluebottles, carefully rinsed,
Are smothered in garlic, and painlessly minced.

Black-eyed bees with stings intact
Add a zesty zing, and that's a fact.

Colorado beetles, ants from Kentucky,
Rhode Island roaches, and if you're unlucky

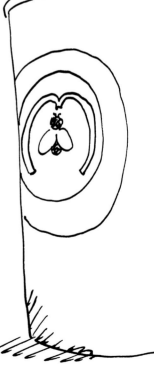

Baltimore bedbugs (and even horrider)
Leeches as squashy as peaches from Florida.

FLIES, FLIES, big juicy FLIES,
FLIES as American as Mom's apple pies.

It's lovely down in MacDingles today
But if you don't fancy flies
Better I'd say to keep well away
Stay home and eat Birds' Eyes.

* Newspaper headline referring to hamburgers being airlifted to
feed homesick US marines.

THE WATERBUG SONG

Said the Water Boatman
To the Water Boatmaid,
'Won't you marry me?
We'll leave this boring pond behind
And sail across the sea.'

Said the Water Boatmaid
To the Water Boatman,
'Thanks, but I've no wish
To leave my natural habitat
And feed the deep-sea fish.'

So the Water Boatman
Set off the next day
To cross the ocean wide.
Some say he lives on a tropical isle
Others say he died.

Said the Water Boatmaid,
'How good to be free
And frail and pretty and young.'
And she sang a wee song
As she drifted along.

And she didn't hear the snap
Of the dragonfly's tongue.

And she didn't hear the snap
Of the dragonfly's tongue.

NEDDY NORRIS AND THE USELESS ANT-EATER

It was two days after the picnic
On which Neddy tortured the ants
That the ghost of the first one haunted him
By climbing up his pants.

The next day a second ant
Bit him on the toe,
The day after this another
Decided to have a go.

There must have been six thousand ants
And the ghost of each one swore
It would nibble Neddy Norris
Till Neddy Norris was no more.

Neddy went into a pet shop
And he bought a tame ant-eater.
He thought with glee: 'Now I'll be safe,
And life will be much sweeter.'

The ant-eater was rather placid –
Though it saw what was going on.
It stared at the ants as they marched past
Without eating a single one.

Neddy continued to be bitten,
He howled and made a din.
His family grew fed up
And threw him in the bin.

Now the ghostly voice of Neddy Norris
Moans at the failure of his plan,
For he never guessed the ant-eater
Was a vegetarian.

BEE'S KNEES

Ever seen a bee slip?
Ever kissed a bee's lip?

Ever felt a bee slap?
Ever sat on a bee's lap?

Ever made a bee start?
Ever eaten a bee's tart?
   (rose petals and honey)

Ever told a bee 'Stop!'?
Ever spun a bee's top?

Ever heard a bee sneeze?
Ever tickled a bee's knees?

Nor me.

SNAIL'S PACE

a snail's face
is not one I'd like to kiss
a snail's pace
g o e s s o m e t h i n g r a t h e r l i k e t h i s
and as for that shell suit!

YUK!

I'd never hug a slug
Or use one as an earplug!

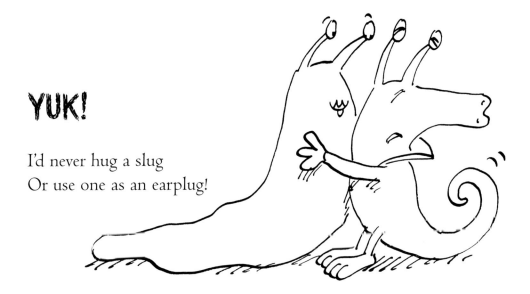

THE SPIDER AND THE LAW

'Spider, spider, you'll never catch
A hawk inside that web.'

'It's made for flies and not for hawks,'
Is what the spider said.

'Spider, spider, why is the law
So like a spider's web?'

'It catches flies, but not the hawks,'
Is what the spider said.

WE'RE STILL AFTER A PET
but we don't know yet
what kind of a pet we should get.

An underwater pet!
What divine inspiration!
So let's put our cozzies on
And head down to the ocean . . .

Now a seal might seem ideal
But where is the appeal
In feeding it smelly fish
For every single meal?

Or what about a whale?
Every day for luncheon
We would have to go and find
A ten-ton tin of plankton!

Beneath the cold blue waves
The creatures are stupendous
Let's dive in and find
One that will befriend us.

CROSS PORPOISES

The porpoises
were looking really cross
so I went over
and talked at them

Soon they cheered up
and swam away
leaving laughter-bubbles
in their wake

It never fails,
talking at cross porpoises.

PEEPSHOW

The ocean's out there
It's vast and it's home
And I want to be in it
With the freedom to roam

Not stuck in a prison
That's made out of glass
For humans to peer into
As they file past,

It's all right for goldfish
And small fry like that
But I deserve more
Than being ogled at

Imagine the look
You'd have on your face
If you had to live
In such a small space

Little wonder
That I look so glum
Banged up in a seaside
Aquarium.

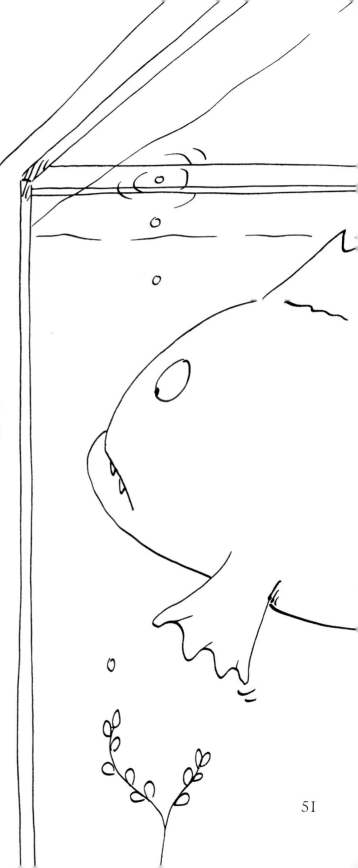

CONGER EEL

Is there
a longer meal
than a
conger eel?

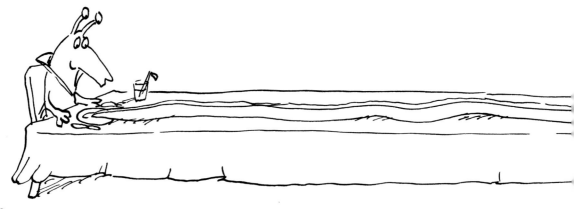

JELLYFISH PIE

Shuna chewed my tuna sandwich
Sammy scoffed my salmon bap
Nigella gnawed my pork panini
Gavin unravelled my Mexican wrap

Petra pecked my pickled pepper
Natalie netted my shrimp-on-rye
Kylie slyly nibbled my bagel
But nobody touched my jellyfish pie.

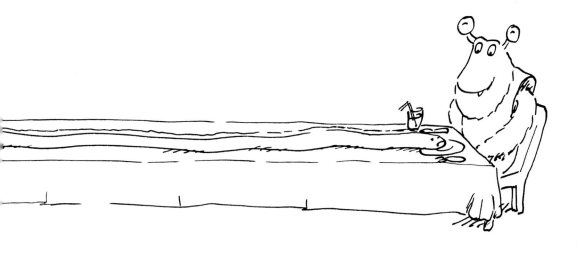

PULL THE OTHER ONE

A crab, I'm told,
     will not bite
or poison you
     just for spite.

Won't lie in wait
     beneath a stone
until one morning,
     out alone

You poke a finger
     like a fool
into an innocent-
     looking pool.

Won't leap out
     and grab your hand
drag you sideways
     o'er the sand

To the bottom
        of the sea
And eat you, dressed
        for Sunday tea.

A crab, I'm told,
        is a bundle of fun
(With claws like that
        Pull the other one.)

SHARK IN THE PARK

Ever see
a shark
picnic
in the park?

If he offers
you a bun

run.

GOLDFISH

Goldfish
are not
boldfish

They cry
when they
fall over

They tittletat
and chew
fat

And are glad
when it's
all over.

THE WET GOLDFISH

'I'm wet,' said the goldfish,
'Please bring me a towel.
Hurry, do as you're told!
I hate all this water
And think I have caught a
Bit of a chill or a cold.'
To the man who sold fish
I said that my goldfish
Was going mad in its bowl.
'It says it hates water
And thinks that I ought to
Go and fetch it a towel.'
'I suppose if you wish
To pamper goldfish
You ought to do as you're told.
But I honestly wish
I'd not sold you that fish,
For it seems quite a rare fish,
And I'd rather not sell fish
Worth double their weight in pure gold.'

TICKLISH

When is a
stickleback
ticklish?

When it's
tickled
with a
little stick
of liquorice.

CLANK

Yesterday at dinner hour
while I was eating fish
I thought about
the fishermen
and made a little wish.
I wish the fish
were silver
to make the fishtanks
clank
which fish
the then rich fishermen
could put in the
Dogger bank.
(Before they sank.)
      Thank you.

WHALES

whales
are floating cathedrals
let us rejoice

cavorting mansions
of joy
let us give thanks

divine temples
of the deep
we praise thee

whaleluja!

THE WHALE'S HYMN

In an ocean before cold dawn broke
Covered by an overcoat
I lay awake in a boat
And heard a whale.

Hearing a song so solemn and so calm
It seemed absurd to feel alarm –
But I had a notion it sang
God's favourite hymn,

And spoke direct to Him.

THE OCEAN'S ONE ALMIGHTY PUDDLE
With nothing to pick up and cuddle . . .

So it's deep into the jungle
Even though we have heard
Some animals might eat us
We're not s-s-s-s-scared

For we may find a pet that's ideal.
 (Unless we end up on the savannah
 as our new pet's meal.)

THE LION AND THE ECHO

The King of the Beasts, deep in the wood,
Roared as loudly as it could.
Right away the echo came back
And the lion thought itself under attack.

'What voice is it that roars like mine?'
The echo replied, 'Mine, mine.'

'Who might you be?' asked the furious lion,
'I'm king of this jungle, this jungle is mine.'
And the echo came back a second time,
'This jungle is mine, is mine, is mine.'

The lion swore revenge if only it could
Discover the intruder in the wood.
It roared, 'Coward! Come out and show yourself!'
But the fearless echo replied simply '. . . elf.'

'Come out,' roared the lion. 'Enough deceit,
Do you fear for your own defeat?'
But all the echo did was repeat,
'Defeat . . . defeat . . .'

Frightened by every conceivable sound
The exhausted lion sank to the ground.
A bird in a tree looked down and it said,
'Dear lion, I'm afraid that what you hear
Is simply the voice of your lion-sized fear.'

THE ASS IN A LION'S SKIN

Dressed up in a lion's skin
An ass, far from bright,
Caused terror to its master
And gave everyone a fright.

Dressed up, it felt important
As it sneaked out late at night
To terrorize the neighbourhood
While it wasn't very light.

One day the ass's master
Threw away his fears.
Sticking through the lion's skin
He saw the ass's ears.

'Stupid creature!' yelled its master.
'Stupid! Dumb! Daft!'
He hit the ass with great relief,
But was nervous when he laughed.

THE DEVIL OF A COOK

I've never cooked a crocodile,
I'm not partial to boiled bear,
I've never fried a fox-cub
(Think of all that fur).

I've never whisked a weasel
Or mashed a mongoose,
I've never poached a pelican
In the bladder of a moose.

I've never sautéd snakes
Or guzzled grilled gazelle,
I've never tried to toast
A tortoise in its shell.

Liquidizing lizards
And microwaving mice
Might be stylish cooking
But they don't taste very nice.

Grating baby glow-worms
Or mincing death's-head moths
Does nothing for my tastebuds.
(I can't stand insect broths.)

Though I've baked a badger
And casseroled a chimp,
Sitting down and eating them
Would make my bowels go limp.

I'm the devil of a cook,
The animals know me well.
I fry their souls for breakfast
In my kitchen down in hell.

UNFAIR

A giraffe's a giraffe,
An ape is an ape,
But a pig is a sausage
In a different shape.

THREE WAYS TO STOP ALLIGATORS FROM BITING YOUR BOTTOM WHEN YOU ARE ON THE TOILET

1) Do not go during the rainy season.

2) If you must go, use only toilets
   in the first-class sections of aeroplanes.

3) Using face paints, make your bottom so scary
   it will frighten them away.

BECOMING A PYTHON'S LUNCHEON
Fills us with revulsion.

The rattle of a rattlesnake
Would only make us twitch and quake.

Cobra's eyes hypnotize, and what a fright
If a boa constrictor picked a fight!

And you'd be madder if an adder chose
To hibernate inside your nose.

We're not brave enough yet
To keep a snake as a pet!

WE'RE ALL GOING TO THE ZOO

We're all going to the zoo
The chimp and the lion
and the kangaroo

The polar bear, the tiger
and the elephant too
We're all going to the zoo

Boo Hoo Boo Hoo Boo Hoo!

A PORCUPINE

A porcupine
      that lost its quills
ran away from home
      and took to the hills

All day long
      it cried as it crawled,
'No one can love
      a creature so bald.'

But it was wrong,

A handsome kestrel
      dropped by to say,
'I Love You! I Love You!'
      Then snatched it away.

HIPPO-RHYME-OPOTOMUS

'I'm sick to death,' the hippo said,
'I tell you, there are times
I'd like to crush those awful poets
And all their silly rhymes.
It is really undignified
The way they rhyme my name.
I wish I was magnanimous
But I feel venomous
When my name's made autonomous
With people like Hieronymous.
It's absolutely scurrilous
How their half-baked rhymes mock at us
Harmless hippopotamus.'

OLD HIPPOS

Old hippos
      one supposes
have terrible
      colds in their noses

Attracted to these
      nasal saunas
germs build their nests
      in darkest corners

Then hang a sign
      that says politely
(streaming, streaming,
      day and nightly)

'Thank you for havin' us
in your nostrils so cavernous.'

THE COMPLACENT TORTOISE

Languid, lethargic, listless and slow,
The tortoise would dally, an image of sloth.
'Immobile!' 'Complacent!' To the hare it was both.

'Enough of your insults, I seek satisfaction.
I'll run you a race and win by a fraction.'
Thus challenged the tortoise one afternoon.
'Right,' said the hare, 'let it be soon.'

They decided they'd race right through the wood
And the tortoise set off as fast as it could.
The hare followed at a leisurely pace
Quite confident it could win the race.

The tortoise thought as it ambled along
'I have never been faster, or quite so strong.'
The hare on the other hand was often inclined
To stop at the roadside and improve its mind.

It read a fable by Aesop deep in the wood
Then of course it set off as fast as it could.
It decided it would put that fable aright
As it sped along with the speed of a light.

Languid, lethargic, listless and slow
The tortoise ran as fast as a tortoise could go.
Yet the hare, having decided on saving face,
Quite easily managed to win the race.

'I feel,' said the tortoise, 'that I've been deceived,
For fables are things I've always believed.
I would love to have won a race so clearly designed
To point out a moral both old and refined.'

'Losing a race would not matter,' the hare said,
'For in speed Mother Nature placed me ahead.
Some fables are things you ought to contest –
Dear tortoise, in mine, I'm afraid you've come last.'

THE GLOOMY TORTOISE

A tortoise called Dorcas thought life ludicrous.
Carrying his own sarcophagus
His life felt endlessly posthumous.

SMALL WONDERS

Brand-new elephants roamed through the jungles.
Brand-new whales splashed down through the oceans.
God had slapped them together,
Happy as a kid making mud pies.

He wiped His hands clean.
'Now for the hard part,' He thought.
He took his workbench into the garden.
Delicately He placed in the bee's sting,
The moth's antenna,

His hand
Not trembling in the slightest.

THE PANTHER'S HEART

Although he still pads about behind
The bars of his solitary cage,
Although he still looks up nightly
At the moonstruck mountains
And the falling snow,
The panther's heart
Stopped long ago.

ZEBRA CROSSING

There is a Lollipopman
At the zebra crossing.
With lollipops
He is trying
To lure zebras across
He makes me cross.
I cross.

PHEW! OUR JOURNEY SO FAR HAS BEEN EXCITING
But we don't want a pet whose hobby is biting!

Cats and dogs come highly recommended;
Could this mean our search has nearly ended?

PETS

Pets are a godsend to people who enjoy the company of
small animals. Cats, for example, are very popular.
As are dogs. We had a dog once called Rover, but he
died. So now we don't call him anything.

ITCHY CAT

Itchy cat, itchy cat where have you been?
To Buckingham Palace to sniff the Queen.
Itchy cat, itchy cat why do that?
Because I was chasing a right royal rat.
But I was polite and I said please,
And I came home with superior fleas.

CERBERUS, THE DOG

Cerberus is not a pet I would get.
Nor is it one I would let
Anywhere near me.
It's scary and hairy:
A three-headed hound,
Each head
The size of a football.
Each mouth
Reeking of decay.
Its six eyes
Red as burst tomatoes.
Its three tails
Coiling and hissing behind it.
If it broke free
One head would swallow the moon,
One head would swallow the sun,
One head would swallow the stars.
No, Cerberus is not
The kind of pet
I would get.

In mythology, Cerberus is the monstrous
watchdog that guards the entrance to the Underworld.

CHUTNEY

A gastronomical cat from Putney
Concocted a wonderful chutney
Bits of old lamb mixed with strawberry jam
Which tasted sweet and yet muttony.

THE INVISIBLE MAN'S INVISIBLE DOG

My invisible dog is not much fun.
I don't know if he's sad or glum.
I don't know if, when I pat his head,
I'm really patting his bum instead.

DOG TALK

Cow says 'Moo'
Duck says 'Quack'
Dog says 'Scrunch my ears
And ruffle my back.'

Pig says 'Oink'
Bird says 'Tweet'
Dog says 'Gimme a bowl
Of biscuits and meat.'

Sheeps says 'Baa'
Horse says 'Neigh'
Dog says 'Get up, lazybones
Let's go out and play.'

Hen says 'Cluck'
Cat says 'Miaow'
Dog says 'OK, I give in,
Woof woof, bow wow.'

BURYING THE DOG IN THE GARDEN

When we buried
the dog in
the garden on
the grave we put
a cross and
the tall man
next door was
cross.
'Animals have no
souls,' he said.
'They must have animal
souls,' we said. 'No,'
he said and
shook his head.
'Do you need a
soul to go
to Heaven?' we
asked. He nodded
his head. 'Yes,'
he said.
'That means my
hamster's not
in Heaven,' said
Kevin. 'Nor is

my dog,' I said.
'My cat could sneak
in anywhere,' said
Clare. And we thought
what a strange place Heaven
must be with
nothing to stroke
for eternity.
We were all
seven.
We decided we
did not want to
go to Heaven.
For that the
tall man next
door is to blame.

PUSSY PUSSY PUDDLE CAT

Pussy pussy puddle cat
what do you think
you're playing at
making puddles
on the mat
chairs and tables
don't do that!

MARMALADE

A ginger tom
name of Marmalade
shaved his whiskers
with a razorblade

Last mistake
he ever made.

COOL CAT

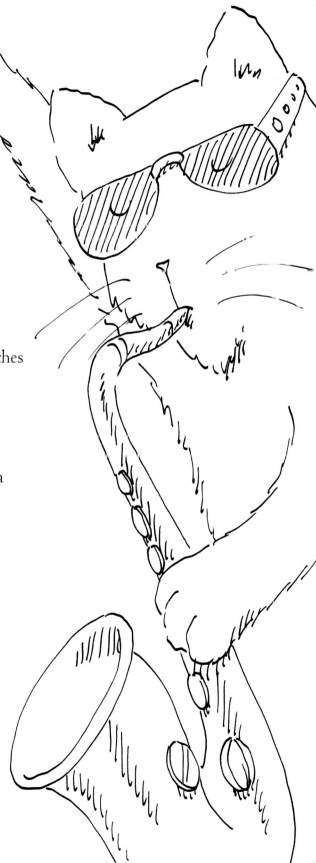

My cat may look like your cat
With know-it-all eyes like yours
Spreadeagling itself on your tummy
To practise sharpening its claws

My cat may look like your cat
With sticky-out whiskers like yours
And the knack of slipping off branches
To land safely each time on all-paws

My cat may sound like your cat
With a pitiful mew like yours
After scratching the arms of the sofa
Tries to burrow under closed doors

My cat may look like your cat
And my cat may sound like yours
But my cat plays the saxophone
And dances to wild applause.

SOMEONE STOLE THE

While I was taking a short   -nap
  someone stole the   ,
I should have spun round like a   herine wheel
  when someone stole the   .
But I was too slow to   ch them,
  when someone stole the   .

Now the   amaran can't float,
  because someone stole the   .
And the   erpillar can't crawl,
  because someone stole the   .
And the   aract can't fall,
  because someone stole the   .

It was not me and it was not you
  but it is   egorically true,
And if you were to ask me
  I'd say it was a   astrophe
That someone's stolen the   .

WE'VE BOTH FOUND A PET!
We're dizzy with success!
What did each of us get?
Can you guess?

Not a tiger or gorilla
Not a hog in a bog
Not a llama or a whale
Or a snake beneath a log.

Not something that wriggles
Or crawls or creeps,
But two magical pets
That we've got for keeps!

One's warm and fluffy
And the other likes to bark.
Mum says they're better
Than a python or a shark.

94

'I think I'll call my puppy Tiddles.'
'I think I'll call my kitten Rover.'
'Or do you think that maybe
We should swap the names over?'

INDEX OF FIRST LINES

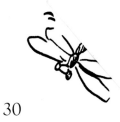